TWELVE LETTERS

TO

YOUNG BELIEVERS

by
EDWARD DENNETT

Published and Distributed

by

THE RALPH E. WELCH FOUNDATION

181 Monterey Road

Orange, California

PREFACE

These letters to young believers are reprinted, without alteration, from the *Christian's Friend* magazine. They were originally written by the editor for the help of one who had but recently been converted, and who had never the opportunity of listening to oral teaching. But inasmuch as the subjects of which they treat are of vital and abiding interest they are now issued in a separate form, with the prayer that the Lord may be pleased to bless them to the edification of many of the lambs of His flock.

BLACKHEATH,

December, 1877.

* * *

Gift copies will be furnished upon request as long as the supply lasts.

THE RALPH E. WELCH FOUNDATION

181 Monterey Road

Orange, California

TWELVE LETTERS
TO
YOUNG BELIEVERS

I.

PEACE WITH GOD

My Dear ———:

You complain that you have not "settled peace," and that thus you are making but little progress with the truth, or in the knowledge of the Lord. The complaint, I am sorry to know, is by no means uncommon; but it springs from an imperfect knowledge of the gospel, and from confounding two different things. I hope therefore, with the Lord's blessing, to be able to help you, if you will carefully consider what I am about to write.

Your case reminds me exactly of another that recently came before me. "Have you peace with God?" I inquired. The answer returned was, "Not always." In both cases the confusion is between the peace made, and the enjoyment of the peace. That is, when you are happy in the Lord you say, "Now I have peace"; but when from failure or trial you are depressed and gloomy, you think that your peace is gone. To meet this state of mind, I shall ask you to consider attentively, *what are the foundations of peace with God.* It is an immense gain to the soul when it is clearly perceived that these lie not within, but without; for then it will also be seen that our experiences have nothing whatever to do with the question. Turn then with me to Romans 5: 1. There we read, "Therefore being justified by faith, we have peace with God through our Lord Jesus Christ"; and if we examine the connection of this scripture, we shall at once learn the source of the peace of which it speaks. The connection is this. After the apostle has explained the way in which Abraham was justified before God, he proceeds: "Now it was not written for his sake alone, that it was imputed to him; but for us also, to whom it shall be imputed, if we believe on Him that raised up Jesus our Lord from the dead; who was delivered for our offences, and was raised again for our justification. Therefore being justified by faith, we have peace with God" (Rom. 4: 23-25; 5: 1).

It is very clear from this scripture *that the sole foundation of peace with God lies in the work of Christ.* In fact, the foundation having thus been laid, God declares that everyone who believes His testimony concerning it, believes that He in grace has come in, and made full provision for the sinner's salvation, *believes thus in God,* is justified, and being justified has—enters upon the possession of—the peace which has been made by the death of Christ. But it will be observed that it is said that Christ was delivered for our offences, *and was raised again for our justification* (Rom. 4: 25). That is, the resurrection of Christ is the abiding proof of the completion of His work, the evidence that the sins for which He died, and under which He went down into death, are gone for ever—the witness therefore that every claim that God had upon us has been fully met and satisfied. For if He was delivered for our offences, and He has left the grave, been raised out of death, the "offences" under which He went down into death must be gone, or He would still be a prisoner in the tomb. Hence the resurrection of Christ is the distinct and emphatic expression of God's satisfaction with the atonement which was made on the cross.

It is thus abundantly evident, as before said, that the alone foundation of peace with God lies in the death of Christ. This is repeated again and again in Scripture. Thus we are said to be "justified by His blood" (Rom. 5: 9); and again, "having made peace through the blood of His cross" (Col. 1: 20). It is therefore Christ who makes peace with God, and He has made it by His sacrificial death—the death that vindicated every claim God had upon the sinner, met every one of His righteous requirements from man, glorified Him in every attribute of His character; so that God now can beseech the sinner to be reconciled to Him (2 Cor. 5: 20).

Having explained this much, it follows that the one important question for the soul is, Do I believe God's testimony concerning His Son, and concerning the work He has accomplished? If there is any difficulty in answering this question, then no further progress can at present be made. A very simple test, however, will help to elicit the truth. On what do you rest for acceptance before God? Is it on yourself, your own doings, or your own merits or deservings? If so, you cannot be resting on the work of Christ. But if you own that by nature you are hopelessly undone and lost, and confess that you have no hope apart from Christ and what He has done, then you can humbly say, "By the grace of God I believe in the Lord Jesus Christ."

Supposing now that you can adopt this language, then I can tell you that you have "settled" peace with God, that nothing can ever deprive you of it— no change, no variety of experience; for it is your immutable, inalienable possession. The Scripture says, "Therefore being justified *by faith*" (and you say you do believe), *"we have peace* with God through our Lord Jesus Christ." Every believer— and the moment he believes—is justified, acquitted of all charge of guilt, and made the righteousness of God in Christ (2 Cor. 5: 21); and being justified, he has peace—not peace in himself, be it observed, but peace *through our Lord Jesus Christ;* that is, the peace which now belongs to him is the peace with God which Christ has made by His atoning sacrifice. And since it is the peace which He has made, being thus outside of ourselves, it can never be altered, and can never fluctuate; it is as stable and as durable as the throne of God; for, as we have seen, it is a peace which Christ has made through the cross; and what He has thus done can never be undone, and therefore it is an everlasting peace. And this abiding, settled, everlasting peace is the portion of every believer.

What you mean, then, when you complain that you have not settled peace, is simply that you do not *enjoy* settled peace, that your experience fluctuates. It may be, therefore, as well to inquire how the believer is to enjoy constant peace in his soul. The answer is very simple. *It is by faith.* If I believe God's testimony that peace is mine on faith in the Lord Jesus, I shall enter immediately on its enjoyment. This may be simplified by an illustration.

Suppose that news is brought to you that by the will of a deceased relative you have become the owner of a large estate. The effect on your mind will depend entirely upon the fact whether or not you believe what you have heard. If you doubt the truth of the news, there will be no answering response to it; but if, on the other hand, it is duly attested, and you implicitly receive it, you will at once say, "The property is mine." So is it also in regard to peace with God. If you believe God's testimony that peace has been made by the blood of Christ, no depression of feeling, no conviction of unworthiness, no circumstances whatever, will be able to disturb your security upon this point, because you will see that it depends entirely upon what another has done. *What is thus needed for the enjoyment of settled peace is unwavering repose upon the word of God.*

The cause of so much uncertainty on this subject springs mainly from looking within instead of looking without to Christ—looking within to discover something that will give confidence that there is a real work of grace begun in the soul, instead of looking without to perceive that the only foundation on which a soul can rest before God is the precious blood of Christ. The consequence is that, perceiving the corruption, the evil of the flesh, the soul begins to doubt whether after all it has not been deceived. Satan thus entangling the soul, plies it with doubts and fears, in the hope of producing distrust of God, if not utter despair. The effectual means of foiling his assaults in this direction is to appeal to the written word. In answer to all his evil suggestions we should reply, as our blessed Lord did when He was tempted, "It is written," and then we should soon find that nothing could disturb our enjoyment of that peace with God which has been made by the precious blood of Christ, and which became ours as soon as we believed.

This foundation question settled, now freed from self-occupation, you will have leisure of mind and soul for meditation upon the truth as revealed in the Scriptures. "As a new-born babe, you will desire the sincere milk of the word, that you may grow thereby" (1 Peter 2: 2) ; and, moreover, if you study the word in the presence of the Lord, you will be guided by it into ever closer intimacy of communion with Himself, and as you trace out His infinite perfections and glories that are unfolded to us and apprehended by the Spirit of God, your affections will be drawn forth in ever increasing fervency, and your heart, now satisfied, will overflow in adoration at His feet, and thus your complaint will be changed into a song of praise.

Believe me, dear ——,

Yours affectionately in Christ,

E. D.

II.

OUR PLACE BEFORE GOD

My Dear ——:

I am a little anxious lest, knowing now that you have peace with God, you should be content, and settle down, thinking that this is all the blessing that God has provided for you in Christ. Many fall into this snare, and thereby never understand the place into which they are brought.

Permit me, then, to remind you, that great as the blessing is, on the enjoyment of which you have entered, it falls infinitely short of God's thoughts and God's desires for you. I may be able to make this more simple, if I direct your attention again to the foundation. The foundation of all lies in the cross of Christ; for it was there that He both met, on our behalf, every claim of God's holiness, and fully glorified Him in every attribute of His character. It is to this He Himself referred when He said, "I have glorified Thee on the earth: I have finished the work which Thou gavest Me to do" (John 17: 4). And it is on this ground, as having thus established a claim upon God, that He prays, "And now, O Father, glorify Thou Me with Thine own self with the glory which I had with Thee before the world was" (v. 5). You will therefore see that God's estimate of the work of Christ is seen in the place which He has accorded to Him at His own right hand. We may even say more: that nothing less than this would have been an adequate response to the claim which Christ had, through His finished work, established on God. And surely nothing less could have satisfied the heart of God; for who shall even imagine His joy in intervening to raise Christ from the dead, setting Him down at His own right hand, and in giving "Him a name which is above every name: that at the name of Jesus every knee should bow, of things in heaven, and things in earth, and things under the earth; and that every tongue should confess that Jesus Christ is Lord, to the glory of God the Father"? (Philip. 2: 9-11). Observe, then, very carefully these three things: first, that the place now occupied by Christ in glory is the fruit of His redemptive work; secondly, that He occupies it as Man; and hence, thirdly, that He is there on behalf of His own. The consequence is, that God must bring us into the same place; that God's glory is concerned in according to believers the same place of acceptance before Him; yea, that His heart delights also to acknowledge thus the work and worthiness of His beloved Son. *Every believer therefore is before God according to the efficacy of the work of Christ, and in all the acceptability of His Person,* and thus enjoys a position of perfect nearness, and is the object of the perfect complacency of God; for he is brought, even now, home to God in Christ Jesus.

I may now lead you to a few scriptures which will abundantly substantiate the above statements. The very next verse to that which occupied our attention in the last letter will do much towards this. "Therefore being justified by faith, we have peace with God through our Lord Jesus Christ"; and then the apostle proceeds: "By whom also we have access by faith into this grace wherein we stand, and rejoice in hope of the glory of God" (Rom. 5: 1, 2). It is thus not only peace with God that we have on believing, but we have access also through Christ into this grace wherein we stand; *i.e.*, we are brought into the full favor of God—into the unclouded sunlight of His presence, and there we can rejoice—everything being settled and secured—in hope of the glory of God. So perfect and so inalienable is the place into which we are brought, on faith in Christ —on faith in Him who raised up Jesus our Lord from the dead—that, notwithstanding the trials, difficulties, and dangers of the wilderness-path, we can rejoice in the hope—in the sure and certain prospect—of the glory of God. There may be, as the apostle goes on to tell us, tribulations; but if so, we can glory even in these, "knowing that tribulation worketh patience; and patience, experience; and experience, hope; and hope maketh not ashamed; because the love of God is shed abroad in our hearts by the Holy Ghost which is given unto us"—that love which God proved, commended toward us, in that, while we were yet sinners, Christ died for us. Having too, while we were yet enemies, been reconciled to God by the death of His Son, much more, we are entitled to conclude, we shall be saved—saved completely, including the redemption of the body (8: 23)—by His life, the life of the risen Saviour at the right hand of God. And not only so, but we also joy in God, through our Lord Jesus Christ, by whom we have now received the reconciliation (see margin) (5: 3-11). Thus we have as our present portion, the love of God shed abroad in our hearts; we joy in Himself, we occupy before Him a place of perfect favor, and rejoice in the hope of the glory of God.

But even this is not all. In this same epistle we are taught, not only that our guilt is gone for ever as soon as we believe in Christ, that we are justified, etc., but we are also shown to be brought through the death and resurrection of Christ into a new place altogether—a place outside of the flesh, because we are "in Christ" before God.   The next section of this epistle, commencing at verse 12 of this chapter, and ending with chap. 8, treats of this subject.   You will thus see that, first of all, everything is traced up either to Adam or Christ, the two heads, the first man Adam, and the second man Christ (5: 12-21). The consequence is, that every one is seen in Adam or in Christ, and I need hardly say, whether we are in Adam or Christ, depends upon whether or not we are believers.   If through grace we are believers, we are in Christ. This being so, there are certain blessed results which I will briefly indicate, leaving you at your own leisure to follow out the subject.

The first thing the apostle reminds us is, that the very ground on which we are—the ground taken at our baptism—shows that we profess to be dead with Christ; and this, as is seen in Col. 3: 3, is true of all believers before God.   If you carefully read Rom. 6 you will at once see that the apostle urges our responsibility on this foundation.   Hence *myself* is gone from God's sight as well as my sins, otherwise the apostle could not say, as he does, "Likewise reckon ye also yourselves to be dead indeed unto sin, but alive unto God through Jesus Christ our Lord" (6: 11).

In the next chapter he teaches that we "also are become dead to the law through the body of Christ," etc.; and this prepares the way, after a discussion of the effect of the application of the law to one who is quickened by the Spirit of God, bringing thereby to light the constant presence of sin in the nature and the utter contrariety between the new nature and the old (7: 13-25), for a full statement of the truth as to the believer. "There is therefore," he proceeds to say, "now *no condemnation* to them which are in Christ Jesus," (8: 1), so complete is the deliverance, as well as forgiveness, which we have in Christ. Nay more; he tells us, "Ye are not in the flesh, but in the Spirit, if so be the Spirit of God dwell in you" (8: 9). He thus shows that the believer's standing is not in the flesh, not in the first man Adam at all, but he is before God in a place which is characterized as being in the Spirit; that is, the Spirit, and not the flesh, characterizes his existence before God, because, in the death of Christ, the believer's evil nature also was judged; for "God sending His own Son in the likeness of sinful flesh, and for sin, condemned *sin in the flesh*" (8: 3). Then, after pointing out further blessed consequences of having the indwelling Spirit, he declares that "all things must work together for good to them that love God, to them who are the called according to God's purpose," since "whom He did foreknow, He also did predestinate to be conformed to the image of His Son, that He might be the firstborn among many brethren," etc. He then asks the question, "If God be for us, who can be against us?" and he answers by reminding us that God, in delivering up His Son to death for us all, has given us the proof that He will freely give us all things. This leads him to the triumphant conclusion that nothing can be laid to the charge of God's elect; that since God Himself has justified them, none can condemn them; that since Christ has died, and has risen again, and is even at the right hand of God to make intercession for us, nothing can ever separate us from the love of God, which is in Christ Jesus our Lord (8: 31-39).

Now it would be a fatal mistake for you to rest in the fifth chapter, if you would know the fulness of God's grace, and the wondrous character of His salvation; for, unless we go on to the eighth chapter, we never know what is true for us and of us before God —the complete and perfect deliverance every believer has, though he may be ignorant of it, in Christ. And it is of the utmost importance that you should see that these blessings which have been indicated are in no way connected with attainment. All that I have pointed out is the portion (whether he knows it or not) of every one who cries "Abba, Father," of every babe in Christ.

But even now there is much more beyond; and if you will turn with me to the Ephesians, I will indicate in a few words—for I am unwilling to prolong this letter—the full character of the believer's place before God. Look, first, at the wonderful expressions in the first chapter: "Blessed be the God and Father of our Lord Jesus Christ, who *hath blessed us with all spiritual blessings in heavenly places in Christ*: according as He hath chosen us in Him before the foundation of the world, *that we should be holy and without blame before Him in love*: having predestinated us unto the adoption of children by Jesus Christ to Himself, according to the good pleasure of His will, to the praise of the glory of His grace, *wherein He hath made us accepted in the Beloved*" (1: 3-6). Look at each of the sentences I have underlined, and you will see how perfect is our place before God. For He *has* blessed us with all spiritual blessings, etc.; it is His purpose that we should be *holy and without blame* before Him in love; and He *has* made us accepted in the Beloved.

In the next chapter we have the steps by which we have been brought into the heavenly places. "God, who is rich in mercy, for His great love wherewith He loved us, even when we were dead in sins, hath quickened us together with Christ, (by grace ye are saved) ; and hath raised us up together, and made us sit together in heavenly places in Christ Jesus," etc. (2: 4-6). Here we are regarded as having been dead in sins; Christ is looked upon in this epistle as having gone down into that condition—dead, as it were, in the place of the sinner; God, being rich in mercy, and acting from His own heart of love, came in, in grace, and quickened us *together with Christ*, and then He raised us up together and seated us together in Christ in the heavenlies; so that He has brought us into His own presence; and hence our present place—our place now, even while we are in the body—is in the heavenlies in Christ Jesus. Nothing short of this expresses the fulness of His grace, or satisfies His own heart.

There is one more scripture I desire to bring before you, and then I have done. "As He is, so are we in this world" (1 John 4: 17). As Christ is at the right hand of God—the delight and joy of God's heart—there in all the perfectness of His person, and in all the sweet savor of His sacrifice, so are we in this world; for we stand not in ourselves but in Christ, and are therefore invested with all His own acceptance and fragrance before God.

The Lord give us to have clearer apprehensions of the place into which, in His unspeakable grace, we are brought in Christ Jesus.

Believe me, dear ——,

Yours affectionately in Christ,

E. D.

III.

OUR PLACE ON EARTH

My Dear ——:

In my last letter I attempted to show you our place—as believers—before God; and now I desire to direct your attention to our place here upon the earth; and we shall see, I think, that this is also connected with Christ. Just, indeed, as we are identified with Christ before God as to standing, so also are we identified with Christ before the world. In other words, we are put in His place down here just as we are in Him before God; and I cannot but think that it would be very helpful to us all to have this truth continually before our souls. But there are two aspects of our place on the earth, both of which are important to be understood; the first in relation to the world, and the second in relation to the "camp"; *i.e.*, organized professing Christianity, which has succeeded in this dispensation to the place of Judaism, as the professing witness for God. (See Rom. 11, and compare Matt. 13.)

1. Our place in relation to the world. The Lord Jesus, speaking to the Jews, said, "Ye are from beneath; I am from above: ye are of this world; I am not of this world" (John 8: 23). Afterwards, when presenting His own before the Father, He said, *"They are not of the world, even as I am not of the world"* (John 17: 16); and you will see that, in the section from the 14th to the 19th verses, He essentially puts His disciples in His own place in the

world, just as in the previous paragraph (from the 6th to the 13th verses) He puts them into His own place before the Father. And they have His place in the world, be it remarked, because they are not of it, even as He was not of it; for having been born again they are no longer of the world. Hence He speaks continually of their having to encounter the same hatred, and the same persecution, as befell Himself. Thus, to cite an example, He says, "If the world hate you, ye know that it hated me before it hated you. If ye were of the world, the world would love his own: but because ye are not of the world, but I have chosen you out of the world, therefore the world hateth you. Remember the word that I said unto you, The servant is not greater than his lord. If they have persecuted me, they will also persecute you; if they have kept my saying, they will keep yours also" (John 15: 18-20). The apostle John in like manner indicates the utter contrast between believers and the world, when he says, "We know that we are of God, and the whole world lieth in wickedness"—or "the wicked one" (1 John 5:19).

But there is more than even yet appears from these weighty scriptures. Every believer is regarded by God as having died and been raised together with Christ (Romans 6; Col. 3: 1-3). He has thus been brought, through the death and resurrection of Christ, as completely, in the view of God, out of the world, as Israel was brought out of Egypt through the Red Sea. Hence he is no longer of it, though he is sent back into it (John 17:18), to be for Christ in the midst of it. Paul therefore could say, while active in service for Christ in the world, "God forbid that I should glory, save in the cross of our Lord Jesus Christ, by whom" (or whereby) "the world is crucified unto me, and I unto the world" (Gal. 6: 14). By the cross of Christ he saw that the world was already judged (John 12: 31); and by the application of the cross to himself he regarded himself as dead—crucified to the world—so that there was separation between the two as complete as death could make it.

To sum up these teachings, then, we see that the Christian while in the world is not of it—he is not of it in the same sense as Christ was not of it, he belongs to another sphere—for if any man be in Christ it is a new creation; he has been, as already seen, brought clean out of it through the death and resurrection of Christ. Hence he is to be wholly separate from it; he is not to be conformed to this world (Gal. 1: 3; Rom. 12: 2) in spirit, habits, demeanor, walk; in everything he is to show that he is not of the world. Even more, by the application of the cross he is to hold himself as crucified to it; and there cannot be any attraction or assimilation between two judged things. But again, he is in the world in the place of Christ; *i.e.*, he is in it for Christ, and as identified with Christ. Consequently he is to witness for Christ, to walk as Christ walked (Phil. 2: 15; I John 2: 6, etc.), and he must expect the same treatment as Christ. Not that we look to be crucified as Christ was; but if we are faithful we shall encounter the same spirit in the world as He did: indeed, in proportion as we are like Christ will be the degree of our persecution; and the fact that believers now meet with so little hatred from the world can only be accounted for from their being so little separate from it.

Before I pass to the other branch of the subject, I cannot but urge upon you the importance of breaking with every link that connects you morally with the world. It needs but little penetration to perceive that the spirit of the world, worldliness, is creeping rapidly over God's assemblies, and vauntingly proclaiming itself even at the table of the Lord. What dishonor, yea, what grief, to Him whose death we are gathered to show forth! And what a call upon all the saints to humble themselves before God, and to seek anew for grace to be more devoted, and more separate, so that the world itself may see that we belong to Him whom it rejected, cast out, and crucified! How many of us have the spirit of Paul, who desired "the fellowship of Christ's sufferings, and to be made conformable to His death" in the view of a glorified Christ, the object of his heart, and the goal of all his hopes? May the Lord restore to us, and all His beloved saints, more of this devotedness to Himself in entire separation from the world.

2. Our place in relation to the "camp." In the epistle to the Hebrews we read, "The bodies of those beasts, whose blood is brought into the sanctuary by the high priest for sin, are burned without the camp. Wherefore Jesus also, that He might sanctify the people with His own blood, suffered without the gate. *Let us go forth therefore unto Him without the camp,* bearing His reproach" (chap. 13: 11-13). Two things are very evident in this passage—the blood of the sin-offering was carried into the sanctuary, and the bodies of the beasts which were sacrificed were burnt without the camp; and the apostle points out that these two things have their correspondences in the death of Christ, the antitype indeed of these offerings. Hence we have the double place of the believer—his place before God being in

the sanctuary, where the blood was carried; and his place on earth being without the camp, where Christ suffered. In other words, as before explained, if we are in Christ before God, identified with Him there in all the savor of His own acceptance, we are also identified with Him on earth in His place of shame, reproach, and rejection. *The place of the believer on earth, therefore, is without the camp;* as the writer of this epistle says, "Let us go forth therefore unto Him without the camp, bearing His reproach."

You will perhaps ask me, What is the camp? In the passage which I have just cited, it is clear, from the whole connection, that it is Judaism. What, then, answers to it now? Judaism was of God, and occupied the place of testimony for Him on the earth. Judaism failed; and after Pentecost, on the final rejection of Christ in the preaching of the apostles, was set aside, and Christianity succeeded to its place, as is taught in Romans 11. The camp, then, now is organized Christianity, the outward professing church—which includes all denominations, from corrupt Roman Catholicism to the smallest sects of Protestantism. On what ground, you may further ask, are we called upon to go outside of this camp? *On the ground of its utter failure as a witness for God.* "He that hath an ear, let him hear what the Spirit saith unto the churches" (Rev. 2: 11, etc.). This is our warrant for, and, indeed, our responsibility of, measuring all that claims to be of God by the written Word; and testing thus all these denominations, they are all convicted of disobedience and failure. For the believer, therefore, who would act according to the mind of God, there remains nothing but to take his place outside of all these, apart from the confusion and error of this evil day, with those who are gathered simply unto the name of Christ, in obedience to His Word. Exodus 33 is very instructive in this connection. When Moses came down from the mount (chap. 32), he found that the whole camp had fallen into idolatry, and after returning to intercede for Israel, he came back with "evil tidings" for the people. And he "took the tabernacle, and pitched it without the camp, afar off from the camp, and called it the tabernacle of the congregation. And it came to pass, that every one which sought the Lord went out unto the tabernacle of the congregation, which was without the camp" (v. 7). Moses acted thus, because he had the mind of the Lord in the presence of the failure of the people; and hence it is that we find in this scene a moral picture of our own times. Let me commend it to your careful consideration.

Enough has now been said to enable you to understand the place of the believer on earth. On the one hand it is to be in separation from the world, and on the other it is without the camp. To occupy it will involve hatred from the former, and reproach from the latter. But if so, we are but more fully identified with our blessed Lord. In Hebrews it is thus called, "His reproach." May we neither shun the one, nor be ashamed of the other; nay, may we be enabled to rejoice when we are counted worthy to suffer shame for His name (Acts 4: 41).

Believe me, dear ——,

Yours affectionately in Christ,

E. D.

IV

THE BODY OF CHRIST

My Dear ——:

There is another question, now demanding your attention, connected with the body of Christ. On the day of Pentecost, an entirely new thing—in the unfolding of the counsels of God—took place; viz., the coming of the Holy Ghost. Up to that period, He had wrought upon the earth; for in every past dispensation there had been quickened souls, and "holy men of God spake as they were moved by the Holy Ghost" (2 Peter 1: 21); but until the Lord Jesus was glorified at the right hand of God, the Holy Ghost as a Person was not on the earth. This is no new theory, but is a matter of distinct statement in the Scriptures. Thus when Jesus stood and cried, on the great day of the feast of Tabernacles, "If any man thirst, let him come unto me, and drink. He that believeth on me, as the scripture hath said, out of his belly shall flow rivers of living water," it is explained, that He spake this "of the Spirit, which they that believe on Him should receive: for the Holy Ghost was not yet [given]; *because that Jesus was not yet glorified*" (John 7: 37-39). The Lord Himself spake to the same effect: "It is expedient for you that I go away: for if I go not away, *the Comforter will not come unto you*," etc. (John 16: 7. Compare John 14: 16, 17, 26; 15: 26, etc.) Passing now onward to Acts 2, we find there the historical record of the descent of the Spirit of God: "And when the day of Pentecost was fully come, they were all with one accord in one place. And suddenly there came a sound from heaven as of a rushing mighty wind, and it filled all the house where they were sitting. And there appeared unto them cloven tongues like as of fire, and it sat upon each of them. *And they were all filled with the Holy Ghost,* and began to speak with other tongues, as the Spirit gave them utterance" (vv. 1-4). Thus was fulfilled the words which the Lord spake to His disciples after His resurrection, "Ye shall be baptized with the Holy Ghost not many days hence." And again, "Ye shall receive power, after that the Holy Ghost is come upon you" (Acts 1: 5, 8).

Now it was by the descent of the Spirit that the Church—the Church of God as found in the New Testament—was formed; and it was formed in two aspects; viz., as the house of God, and as the body of Christ. (See 1 Timothy 3: 15, and Ephesians 1: 22, 23). It is the latter of these two aspects which I desire to bring before you in this letter. Two scriptures will clear our way. In Col. 1: 18 we read, "And He is the head of the body, the Church": in 1 Cor. 12: 13, "For by one Spirit are we all baptized into one body, whether we be Jews or Gentiles, whether we be bond or free," etc. It thus appears that, on the day of Pentecost, by the descent of the Holy Spirit, believers were baptized into one body, and that thus the body of Christ was formed.

Let me, then, now inquire of what or of whom the body of Christ is composed. "As the body is one, and hath many members, and all the members of that one body, being many, are one body: *so also is Christ*" (1 Cor. 12: 12). The term Christ, as here used, includes Christ Himself and all the members of the body, looked at as a complete whole. Hence the body of Christ includes Himself as the Head, and all believers on earth who have received the indwelling Spirit; and consequently every child of God who can cry, "Abba, Father," is a member of the body of Christ. The apostle thus says, "We are members of His body, of His flesh, and of His bones" (Eph. 5: 30).

This is the point I would press upon your attention; for vast numbers of God's beloved children are in ignorance of this wonderful place and privilege. Thus, in a visit I made some time ago to a dying believer, I said, "Do you know that you are a member of the body of Christ?" The answer was, "No; I never heard of that"; and I shall not soon forget the joy that overspread that dying countenance as I unfolded the scriptures bearing upon this subject. Let me, then, ask you to consider what being a member of the body of Christ involves. First, and foremost, it teaches us that we are united to Christ—to Christ as a glorified man, at the right hand of God. For inasmuch as He is the Head of the body, every member is vitally and (may we not say?) organically united to Him. He that is joined to the Lord is one spirit (1 Cor. 6: 17). See then the vast extent of the grace of our God! It is not only that our sins are forgiven, that we are justified by faith, that we are brought into the perfect unclouded favor of God, that we are risen with Christ, that we are seated in Him in the heavenlies; but even, as down here upon the earth, encompassed by weakness and infirmity, it is given us to know that we are united to Christ in glory. We can look up to Him where He is, and say, "We are members of His body, of His flesh, and of His bones." How could there be discussions upon the question, whether we may know our safety now, if this truth were known in power? And what strength it would give us all, in the presence of trials or dangers, never so great, if we had this thought before our souls, We are united to Christ. And oh, what a revelation it gives us of the nearness and the intimacy into which we are brought with Him! for we are made to know that we are one with Himself, that whatever touches us touches Him (see Acts 9: 4); and therefore that we are inseparably, indissolubly, connected with Himself for ever.

Secondly, we are taught that being members of the body of Christ, we are also members one of another; and it is essential for us to apprehend this truth, if we would understand the character of our relationships with all the children of God. The same bond, then, that unites us to Christ, unites us also to all believers; for the same Spirit that unites us to Christ has united us also one to another. This is what is meant by "the unity of the Spirit" (Eph. 4: 3); i.e., the unity of all the members of Christ which has been formed on the earth by the Spirit of God.

If you will now turn with me to 1 Cor. 12, you will see the wonderful character of our mutual relationships, arising out of our being members one of another. You can read the passage from the 12th to the 27th verse, at your leisure; in the meantime I will point out several distinctive points in its teaching. First, it is carefully insisted upon that "the body is not one member, but many"; and that every member has its own place in the body. Hence the apostle asks, "If the foot shall say, Because I am not the hand, I am not of the body; is it therefore

not of the body?" And he is careful to show that
the peculiar place which each has in the body is the
result of the sovereign act of God; and he is also
careful to guard us from forgetting, that while there
are many members, it is yet but one body (vv.
14-20). If we had no further instruction, what a
fruitful theme for amplification. But I will only call
your attention here to two points; viz., our obliga-
tion or responsibility to maintain the diversity of
the members (v. 14), and secondly, the unity of the
whole (v. 29); and I venture to add that it is impossible to maintain either the one or the other, ex-
cepting you are gathered, apart from all denominations and human systems, to the name of Christ outside the camp. The second thing is, that every
member of the body *needs* all the other members;
for "the eye cannot say unto the hand, I have no
need of thee: nor again the head to the feet, I have
no need of you"; and he tells us that God hath thus
"tempered the body together," etc., *"that there
should be no schism in the body; but that the members should have the same care one for another"*
(vv. 21-25). He then reminds us that the relationship between the members is so intimate that if "one
member suffer, all the members suffer with it"; and
that if "one member be honored, all the members rejoice with it" (v. 26).

You will see from this scripture, that the term
"the body of Christ" is no mere figure of speech, as
is so often alleged; but that it expresses a reality—
the reality indeed of our union with Christ, as also
of our union with one another. And I am sure that
you will see that our responsibilities to Christ as the
Head of the body, and our responsibilities to our
fellow-members, cannot even be understood, much

less discharged, if this truth is overlooked or ignored. But, on the other hand, when it is known, not only have we the joy of conscious union with Christ; but we can also rejoice in our union, our indissoluble union, with all the members of His body in all parts of the world. It leads moreover to very practical results. For example, if I am asked to connect myself with any of the denominations around, I instantly reply that I cannot do that which denies, plainly denies, this blessed truth. "You ask me," I should say, "to join a certain number of Christians who agree upon certain things; but I am united to all believers, and I need them all, and I cannot therefore accept a ground of union which excludes any." Again, if it is proposed to me to unite with a number of Christians irrespective of denominations, I should answer, "I am a member of the body of Christ; and I cannot therefore make any ground of union apart from that of the body. *I must be on God's ground or upon none at all.*" Until therefore I know the truth of the body of Christ, I cannot understand the place which the Lord would have me to occupy upon the earth.

But I will now leave the subject for your own consideration; for I am sure that if you search the Scriptures, in dependence on the Lord, He will guide you by His Spirit into His own mind respecting it. In my next letter, God willing, I shall bring before you another subject, closely related to this; viz., that of the Lord's table.

Believe me, dear ——,

Yours affectionately in Christ,

E. D.

V.

THE LORD'S TABLE

My Dear ——:

The question of the Lord's table is often a most perplexing one to the child of God. Not only are there many tables, set up on different grounds, around him on every hand, but also, when he begins to enquire into the subject, he finds almost as many theories as tables, concerning the significance of the supper of which he is invited to partake. His only remedy therefore, if he desires to avoid error and to be found in obedience to his Lord, is to turn away from the confused voices of theologians to the clear and distinct teaching of the word of God. It is to this teaching I desire to lead you in this letter.

As we might expect, there is nothing wanting on such a subject in the Scriptures. Thus 1 Cor. 10 explains the character of the table, and chap. 11 gives us the character of the supper, and the manner in which it should be eaten.

First we will consider the question of the table. "The cup of blessing which we bless, is it not the communion of the blood of Christ? The bread which we break, is it not the communion of the body of Christ? For we [being] many are one bread, [and] one body: for we are all partakers of that one bread" (1 Cor. 10: 16, 17). This scripture evidently teaches two things; first, that the loaf or "the bread" on the table is a symbol of the body of Christ ("for we being many are one bread, one body"—see also 1 Cor. 12: 13); and secondly, that we partake of it as members of that body ("for we are all partakers of that one bread"). As therefore we have com-

munion of the blood of Christ through the wine, so
also of the body of Christ through the bread, when
we partake according to the thoughts of God. *The
table is thus the expression of the unity of the body
of Christ; and consequently it is only the members
of that body who can be properly gathered around it.*
The "church" of England, strangely enough, agrees
with this principle; for it admits no one to its table
who has not been baptized; and it declares that every
baptized one is made "a member of Christ," etc.
The error, you will see, lies in attributing to baptism
(as the means) what can only be wrought by the
Spirit of God. I cite this case only to show you that
the principle affirmed, so far from being peculiar,
is widely accepted.

Now, it is by the application of this principle that
you can decide which of all the tables around you is
the Lord's. Test every denominational table by it,
and what is the result? You will perceive at once
that no sectarian system can have the Lord's table,
because the ground on which it is spread, in every
case, is narrower than that of the body of Christ.
Admitting, or rather conceding for the moment, that
all its followers may be members of the body of
Christ, we should still have to say, Are there no
other members of that body outside this denomina-
tion? If there are, then such a table, however sin-
cerely, conscientiously, and piously spread, is not
the table of the Lord. Should it be replied, "But we
are quite willing to receive all other members of the
body of Christ," I should have to answer, "This
does not affect the question at all; for the *ground
taken* determines the character of the table spread
upon it; and the ground taken in each denomina-
tion is of such a character that many godly Chris-

tians could not have fellowship with it." The dissenter*, for example, is shut out, for conscience sake, from the table of the Anglican "church*"; and the Anglican* is similarly excluded from the tables of dissent*; and hence, neither in the one nor the other can the Lord's table be discovered, as the ground taken is other than that of the body of Christ.

Once more, test many of the unsectarian tables by this principle. You may perhaps tell me that you know of a place where all denominationalism is disavowed, and where it is taught that all Christians, and none but Christians, should be united. Very good; but I still should have a few questions to ask. I should inquire, Are the believers in such a place gathered simply unto the name of Christ? Is there liberty in the Spirit to minister by whom He wills? Is there the exercise of godly discipline? etc. For the Lord cannot sanction anything which is not in accordance with the Scriptures—anything which is unsuited to the character of His own name. If these questions could be answered in the affirmative, then you might perhaps conclude, that you had found the Lord's table; but if not, however fair and inviting it might seem at the first, you would have to reject it equally with those in the denominational systems around.

If we add a few characteristics of the Lord's table, it may serve to preserve you from mistake. 1. The table must be spread on ground outside of all denominational systems, otherwise, as we have shown, it could not comprehend all the members of the body of Christ. 2. The saints should be gathered on the

---

* The Church of England is often referred to in England as the Anglican Church; all other Protestants are called dissenters.

first day of the week around the table. We thus read: "Upon the first day of the week, when the disciples came together to break bread" (Acts 20:7), an undeniable proof that it was their custom. See too in John 20, how our blessed Lord, on two occasions after His resurrection, chose the first day of the week for presenting Himself in the midst of His gathered disciples (vv. 19, 26), thus consecrating (if such a word may be used) this day for their assembling to show forth His death. 3. The purpose of the gathering should be to break bread. I point this out, as in many places there is a weekly table, but altogether in subordination to other things, such as preaching, etc. 4. Everything in connection with the table—worship, ministry, and discipline, must be in accordance with, and in subjection to, the word of God. If there is a single human regulation, on whatever ground adopted, the character of the table is destroyed. For it is the table of *the Lord;* and hence His authority alone can be recognized by His gathered saints.

Need I add more? But there is a danger or two which I would fain indicate. The first is indifference. It was only the other day that I asked a believer if she were at the *Lord's* table. Apprehending my meaning, she replied, "It is enough for me to know that Christ is my Saviour, and I do not desire to trouble myself with such questions as these." Can anything be more sad? As if it was not of all-importance to ascertain the mind of the Lord; for surely if He has indicated His will upon this question, it should be our joy to discover it, and to be found in obedience to it. Another replied in a different way. He said, "I am not called upon to judge my fellow-believers, and I desire to have fellowship

with all." "He that hath an ear, let him hear what
the Spirit saith unto the churches" (Rev. 2, 3). We
are thus called upon to judge *the ways* of our fellow-believers—indeed of the "churches"; to measure everything by the Word; and to refuse all which
it does not sanction, or which it condemns. Indifference is that spirit of Laodiceanism concerning
which our Lord says, "So then because thou art
lukewarm, and neither cold nor hot, I will spue thee
out of my mouth" (Rev. 3: 16). The other danger
is that of association. For example, how many a
young believer is led unwittingly into that which is
contrary to the Lord's mind from friendly, relative,
or even spiritual associations! He is guided by the
opinions of his friends, etc., instead of the word of
God; or it may be that, having been converted or received blessing in a particular place, he naturally
desires to continue where the blessing was received.
But the question in every case should be, "Lord,
what wilt thou have me to do?" (Acts 9: 6). Otherwise he might, in the right desire, according to the
Lord's own word, to remember Him in His death,
be found doing it in a way which is really displeasing
to Him.

Warning you against these dangers, let me remind
you that it is far better to wait than to partake of
the Lord's Supper in disobedience. Before therefore
you seek admission to the table, search the Scriptures, looking to the Lord for guidance; "and if thine
eye is single, thy whole body shall be full of light."

Reserving the question of the supper for another
letter,

> Believe me, dear ——,
> Yours affectionately in Christ,
> E. D.

VI

THE LORD'S SUPPER

My Dear ——:

It must never be forgotten that it is possible to be at the Lord's Table, and yet to fail altogether in participating in the Lord's Supper. Thus the Corinthians were gathered out to the name of Christ; they were assembled week after week at the Lord's Table, and yet St. Paul, writing to them, says, "When ye come together therefore into one place, this is not to eat the Lord's Supper" (1 Cor. 11: 20). They had fallen into such disorder, through selfishness, and forgetfulness of the import of the supper, that they had made this solemn occasion a time of feasting. What they were eating therefore was their own, and not the Lord's Supper; for they had dissociated the bread and wine from almost all connection with the body and blood of Christ. Hence the solemn admonition, "What! have ye not houses to eat and drink in? or despise ye the church of God, and shame them that have not? What shall I say to you? shall I praise you in this? I praise you not" (v. 22). Thereon, the apostle proceeds to explain the true character of the supper, and tells us that he had received a special communication concerning it from the Lord. It is of importance to mark this, because, as the apostle received this in connection with his ministry of the body of Christ (Col. 1: 24, 25), and since this is the final communication on the subject, it is to this scripture rather than to the gospels (which, however, relate the institution of the supper on the passover night) that we turn for the exposition of its meaning.

And who can fail to be struck with the wondrous grace displayed in the opening words of this account, "That the Lord Jesus, *the same night in which He was betrayed*, took bread," etc.? (v. 23). What a contrast between the heart of man, and the heart of Christ! About to be betrayed by one of His disciples, "He took bread: and when He had given thanks, He brake it, and said, Take, eat: this is my body, which is broken for you: this do in remembrance of me" (vv. 23, 24).

The bread therefore is a symbol of the body of the Lord Jesus which was given for His own—given up to death for them, for us, for all believers—on the cross; and when we eat it, we are to remember Him. Attention to the word "remember" would save from many mistakes. We remember a thing that is past; *i.e.*, we recall it to mind. So when we eat the bread at the Lord's Supper, we recall the fact that the Lord was once *dead;* we remember Him in that condition —the condition of death—down into which He went, when He bore our sins in His own body on the tree —when He endured all the wrath that was due to us, and so glorified God even about our sin. It is therefore not Christ as He now is, but Christ as He then was, whom we remember in the breaking of bread.

The cup also sets forth the same thing. "After the same manner also He took the cup, when He had supped, saying, This cup is the new testament [covenant] in my blood: this do ye, as oft as ye drink it, in remembrance of me. For as often as ye eat this bread, and drink this cup, ye do shew the Lord's death till He come" (vv. 25, 26). The wine, then, of which we partake is an emblem of the blood of Christ; and this in itself speaks also of death, for we cannot think of blood, as apart from the body, except in connection with death. Indeed, verse 26 emphasizes the truth that, both in eating the bread and drinking the cup, we show, announce, or proclaim, the death of the Lord. We cannot too earnestly insist upon this, that in the Lord's Supper we look back to a dead Christ; that we take it in remembrance of the fact that He once was lying dead—dead on the cross, and dead in the sepulchre; because He not only bore our sins, but was *made sin*—He who knew no sin—that we might be made the righteousness of God in Him. Note well that it is not even a dying, but a dead Christ—not a dying Christ, a continual repetition of His sacrifice, as so many erroneously teach, but a dead Christ; "for by one offering He hath perfected for ever them that are sanctified" (Heb. 10: 14).

This, then, is the one thought which should be before our souls at the Lord's table. What simplicity; but how calculated to touch and bow our hearts in adoration before Him, as, seated around His table, we thus commemorate His death! For "the apostle shows us, if it is a dead Christ, who it is that died. Impossible to find two words, the bringing together of which has so important a meaning, the *death* of the *Lord*. How many things are comprised in that He who is called the Lord had died! What love! what purposes! what efficacy! what results! The Lord gave Himself up for us. We celebrate His death."

And observe, it is "until He come." While therefore we look back to the cross, we are reminded of His coming in glory to receive us unto Himself, the fruit surely of His travail and death; and thus we can never forget that our complete redemption, being "conformed to the image of His Son," is the result of the death of Christ. For the two things, the cross and the glory, are here bound indissolubly together.

Such then is the meaning of the supper; and, as you will perceive, the apostle gives us very solemn warnings against forgetfulness of its import. "Whosoever shall eat the bread, and drink the cup of the Lord unworthily, shall be guilty of the body and blood of the Lord. But let a man examine himself, and so let him eat of that bread, and drink of that cup. For he that eateth and drinketh unworthily, eateth and drinketh damnation [judgment] to himself, not discerning the Lord's body" (vv. 27-29). There is no question here of being ourselves *worthy* to partake of the Lord's Supper; but what the apostle deprecates is "partaking in an unworthy manner. Every Christian, unless some sin had excluded him, was worthy to partake, because he was a Christian. But a Christian might come to it without judging himself, or appreciating as he ought, that which the supper brought to his mind, and which Christ had connected with it. He did not discern the Lord's body; and he did not discern, did not judge, the evil in himself." And if he thus ate and drank, he would eat judgment to himself; *i.e.*, he would bring down discipline upon himself; for the Lord judges His people, chastens them, that they should not be condemned with the world (v. 32). He had thus chastened the Corinthians for their careless ways—some with weakness, some with sickness, and some even with bodily death (v. 30). Hence the necessity of examining ourselves as to the manner in which we partake of the Lord's Supper, and of judging every thing which is thus discovered that is unsuited to the presence of the Lord; "for if we would judge ourselves, we should not be judged" (v. 31); *i.e.*, exercising self-judgment, we should not then be chastened of the Lord.

From all that has been said, it is clear that we are not qualified for the Lord's table until the question of our relationship with God is settled—until, in a word, we have peace with God. For if I am occupied with self, with my own state of soul, with doubts, anxieties, or fears, I cannot be occupied with the death of Christ. Much injury is thus often done in bringing souls too soon to the table; for, coming before they have peace with God, they look upon the table as a means of grace; and inasmuch as the death of Christ is brought before them, they are made, not knowing the value of that death for themselves, wretched and miserable. Until there is peace of conscience through the blood, to say the least, the soul is not free, not at leisure to contemplate the death of Christ.

Once more. When we are at the table, it is not to be occupied with the benefits which we have received through the death of Christ. It is rather to enter, by the power of the Spirit, into God's thoughts concerning the death of His beloved Son. For we are there as worshippers, and as such inside the rent veil, and there we are engrossed with the fact that God Himself was glorified in the death of Christ; and as in fellowship with Himself, we think of what Christ was to Him, how that He was never more precious to Him than in that awful moment when He was made sin, that it was for God's glory He endured all, was obedient unto death, even the death of the cross, then it is with overflowing hearts we are enabled by the Spirit to pour forth our adoration and praise. Wondrous thought, that we should thus be admitted to behold with God His Christ brought down into the dust of death, with all God's waves and billows passing over Him! And as we behold we cannot but cry, "Unto Him that loved us, and washed us from our sins in His own blood, and hath made us kings and priests unto God and His Father; to Him be glory and dominion for ever and ever. Amen" (Rev. 1: 5-6).

We are thus at the table as givers, not as receivers; though surely we do receive when there according to God. But the object of our assembling is to worship, to render the homage of our hearts to God, because we have been redeemed through the death of His Son. And who could describe the blessedness of the privilege of showing in this way the Lord's death? Gathered around Himself, with the touching emblems of His body and blood before our eyes, thus claiming the affections of our hearts, His love, which the many waters could not drown, nor the floods quench, penetrates and possesses our souls, and constrains us to bow in willing adoration at His feet, and makes us long for the time when we shall see Him face to face, and beholding His glory, be with Him, and worship Him throughout the ages of eternity.

Praying that you may be taught more and more of the meaning of His death as set forth in the supper,

Believe me, dear ——,

Yours affectionately in Christ,

E. D.

VII.

THE LORD JESUS CHRIST
IN THE MIDST

My Dear ———:

It is very important for you to have a clear conception of the presence of the Lord in the midst of the assembly; but the condition on which His presence is promised ought never to be forgotten. He has never said that He is *wherever* saints are assembled; that all alike who professedly meet for worship can reckon upon His promise. His words are: "Where two or three are gathered together in my name, there am I in the midst of them." Thus the essential condition is that saints should be "gathered together in His name"; and unless this is fulfilled the promise clearly is not binding.

Our first aim then must be to explain what this condition means. I may say that the more correct translation would be *"unto* my name"; for the preposition which is rendered "in," is one that invariably has the significance of "into" or "unto." Here therefore "unto" will be its sense. Again, it may be needful to point out that that name is not used merely as an appellation, but, as is usual in Scripture, is expressive of all that Christ is in this connection. Thus when the Lord, speaking before the Father of His disciples, says, "I have declared unto them thy name, and will declare it" (John 17: 26), He does not mean that He had merely revealed to them that God also bore the name of Father; but that He had been teaching them all that God was to them in that relationship. Hence He adds, that He had done and would do this, "that the love wherewith thou hast loved me may be in them, and I in them." What He desired therefore was that they should both know what God was to them as the Father, and that they should be brought into the enjoyment of all the love which He had for them as such. In like manner, "name" in the passage before us expresses all that Christ is as the glorified man and Lord in the relationship which He now sustains towards His people. I say "which He *now* sustains"; for it is very evident that these words look on to the time when He should be absent. Thus in Matt. 16 He says, "I will build my church" (v. 18), pointing on to a future time; and the passage in which the word "name" occurs is in connection with church action (v. 17). Indeed, while He was upon the earth the disciples could not be gathered to His name; for they were with Him as their Master and Lord.

We may then take the "name" to be expressive of the person of Christ—Himself, indeed, in all the truth of His person, as the risen and glorified One at the right hand of God. It is clear therefore that Christ is the only object that draws us together, and our centre when gathered; for the Holy Ghost will never gather believers to anything but Christ. If anything is added—whether it be a particular doctrine, or a particular form of church government—it is not simply the name of Christ, and the gathering is not according to His mind. If, for example, I agreed to meet with certain other believers of like views, we could not be gathered alone to the name of Christ, for something has been added or excluded; but if I am gathered with those who acknowledge that Christ Himself is the only attraction, with those who own His authority as Lord, who bow to His word, and regulate everything by it when assembled, then the gathering would be to His name. And only then; for where man's authority, man's traditions, or man's regulations are recognized, whatever the individual piety of those who recognize them, the meeting cannot be of this character.

Now it is in the midst of His people so gathered that the Lord has promised to be. "There am I in the midst of them." This very fact shows the extreme importance of being gathered unto His name; for, as we have said, if the condition be disregarded, we have no ground for reckoning upon His presence. Nor is it enough to *say* that we fulfil the condition. The essential point is, Does the Lord recognize it as fulfilled? He is the Judge; and therefore it were presumption indeed to expect Him in our midst if. assembled according to our own thoughts—without respect to His word. But "where two or three are gathered together in my name, *there am I in the midst of them.*"

We know therefore that He is in the midst of such on the authority of His own word. Not only so; but, as if to meet us in our weakness, He has given us a sample of the manner in which He comes into the midst of His own. Thus on the evening of that first day of the week, when He arose from the dead, the disciples were found assembled together (John 20: 19). He had sent Mary to His "brethren" with this message: "I ascend unto my Father, and your Father; and to my God, and your God" (v. 17). According to Psalm 22, He thus declared God's name unto His brethren, and in so doing revealed that He brought them through His death and resurrection into His own place before God. Hence-forward His God and Father was their God and Father. They were thus associated with Him on resurrection ground in these relationships. This message gathers them together unto His name; and when thus assembled, "He came and stood in the midst, and said unto them, Peace be unto you." Thereby He has given us an example of the manner in which He comes into the midst of His people, so that we might have the certainty of His word veri-fied to our souls.

Should any one therefore be tempted to say, Is it possible that the Lord should be in the midst of His people when gathered now unto His name? the doubt is anticipated by this striking record of His presence in the midst of His disciples on the first day of the week. It meets, indeed, a greater diffi-culty and a more subtle danger. One might be in-clined in unbelief to object, If now we could see Him with our eyes as they did, then we could receive it. The Lord knew the weakness and the subtlety of our poor feeble hearts, and thus in tender love has provided for this snare. One of the disciples, Thomas, "was not with them when Jesus came. The other disciples therefore said unto him, We have seen the Lord. But he said unto them, *Except I shall see* in His hands the print of the nails, and put my finger into the print of the nails, and thrust my hand into His side, *I will not believe*" (v. 25). Eight days after, all, including Thomas, were once more assembled, and, as on the former occasion, "came Jesus, the doors being shut, and stood in the midst, and said, Peace be unto you. Then saith He to Thomas" (for He had heard every word which Thomas had uttered), "Reach hither thy finger, and

behold my hands; and reach hither thy hand, and
thrust it into my side: and be not faithless, but
believing." Thomas, overwhelmed by His tender
grace, and the sense of his own sinfulness, could only
exclaim, "My Lord and my God." Thereupon
"Jesus saith unto him, Thomas, because thou hast
seen me, thou hast believed: blessed are they that
have not seen, and [yet] have believed" (vv. 24-29).
Thus the Lord had those in view (without entering
now into the application of this scene to the conver-
sion of the Jewish remnant, when they shall by-and-
by look on Him whom they have pierced) who
should believe through the word of His disciples, and
pronounces their greater blessedness. And this
blessedness is ours; for though we see Him not, we
believe that, according to His own word, He is in
our midst when gathered unto His name.

It should be remembered, moreover, that it is *He
Himself* who is in the midst—not "in spirit," as is
often said, but He Himself; for the words are,
"There am *I*," and the term *"I"* expresses all that
He is. Christ then—not the Holy Ghost, but Christ
—is in the midst of His gathered saints. The Holy
Ghost acts through the individual members of the
body of Christ, ministering for the edification of
the saints by whom He will, and dwells in the house
of God; but it is Christ, I repeat, who comes into
our midst. His presence is only apprehended by
the Spirit; that is another thing. But He is in the
midst, whether apprehended or not, where two or
three are gathered unto His name. How wondrous
His condescension and grace!

Never forget therefore that it is around the Lord
Himself that we are gathered. If there be only two
—for His words are, "Where two or three are gath-

ered together in my name"—there He is in the midst
of them. As soon as two are thus met, they can rejoice in the knowledge that the Lord is there. Our
faith may be weak, and our apprehension feeble, but
the fact of His presence remains; for it is not dependent upon our feelings or experiences, but solely
upon our being gathered unto His name. How could
we forsake the assembling of ourselves together, as
the manner of some is (Heb. 10: 25), if we remembered that the Lord is the centre of the assembly;
that He is as truly in our midst as with the disciples on the first resurrection day? For why was
Thomas absent on that first occasion? Because he
did not believe in the resurrection of his Lord, and
therefore did not expect His presence. So now, if
any absent themselves (I do not speak of those
whom the Lord detains by affliction, duty, or other
circumstances) from the assembly, it can only be
because they do not really believe in the fact of the
Lord's presence in the midst. And when assembled,
what reverence, what affection, what worship would
be begotten in our hearts, if through the power of
the Spirit of God we more fully apprehended that
He who went down into death under our sins, and
has thereby redeemed us to God by His blood, has
come back out of death, and now, as the risen and
glorified One, delights to come and to lead the praise
of His people in the midst of the congregation. (Ps.
22: 22).

Praying that the Lord may lead you into the
power of this truth,

Believe me, dear ——,

Yours affectionately in Christ,

E. D.

VIII.

THE TRUE PLACE OF WORSHIP

My Dear ——:

In this letter I propose to inquire, Where is the Christian's place of worship? I need scarcely remind you that the term "place of worship" abounds on every hand; and while I fully admit that what is meant thereby is simply the place where believers and others congregate on Lord's-days, yet it is of the· first importance in divine things that words should not be used which convey a wrong impression, or which falsify the truth of God. Our only resource, therefore, is to obtain the answer to our question from the Scriptures.

Let me, then, direct your attention to the following passage: "Having therefore, brethren, boldness to enter into the holiest by the blood of Jesus, by a new and living way, which He hath consecrated for us, through the veil, that is to say, His flesh; and [having] an High Priest over the house of God; let us draw near," etc. (Heb. 10: 19-22, etc). Now, we have in this scripture, to speak generally, three things—the blood of Jesus, the rent veil, and the High Priest (literally, the *great* priest) over the house of God; and it is on the foundation of these three things that we have the exhortation to draw near for worship. If we examine a little the significance of each, the answer to our question will be unfolded.

First, then, we have boldness to enter into the holiest *by the blood of Jesus*. It is evident, if you trace down the argument of the apostle, that the blood of Jesus is brought in as a contrast with "the blood of bulls and goats" (v. 4). Indeed, the whole point of the first part of the chapter is the efficacy of the former in contrast with the impotency of the latter. The fact that the sacrifices under the old dispensation were offered year by year continually, is adduced to prove that the worshippers were never really purged, so as to have no more conscience of sins; for in the repetition of the sacrifices there was a remembrance again made of sins every year (vv. 1-3). And the reason of this was that *"it is not possible* that the blood of bulls and goats should take away sin" (v. 4). Thus the multitude of sacrifices of all kinds did but demonstrate their utter powerlessness, though appointed by God in view of-the One Sacrifice which was thereby foreshadowed.

Having then shown this, the apostle now brings out in sharpest contrast the value of the sacrifice of Christ (read carefully from the 5th to the 14th verses) ; and he sums it up, and states it, in one sentence: "By one offering He hath perfected for ever them that are sanctified." The offerings under the law never made the worshippers perfect. By one offering Christ has perfected us for ever. This truth is so vast and comprehensive that it needs to be meditated upon again and again, in order in any measure to be apprehended. For it implies, not only that I have now no more conscience of sins— if I am under the value of the sacrifice of Christ— but also that I never need have any more conscience of sins in the aspect here presented; that through the efficacy of that precious blood I have a title now, and ever shall have a title, to the presence of God; that nothing, in short, can ever deprive me of the place which it gives me in His own immediate presence; for by one offering He hath *perfected for ever* them that are sanctified. *Through that sacrifice therefore I have received a perpetual qualification for access to God.*

The second thing is the rent veil. The blood of Christ has given us the title to approach; and in the next place we have "a new and living way, which He hath consecrated for us, through the veil, that is to say, His flesh." Here again we have a contrast with the old dispensation. Thus in chap. 9 we read: "Into the second" (*i.e.*, into the holy of holies, behind the veil) "went the high priest alone once every year, not without blood, which he offered for himself, and for the errors of the people: the Holy Ghost thus signifying, *that the way into the holiest of all was not yet made manifest, while as the first tabernacle was yet standing.*" etc. (vv. 7-9). The people were therefore entirely excluded; and this was because, as we have seen, it was not possible that the blood of bulls and of goats should take away sin. It would consequently have been certain death, by the judgment of God, had any one beside the high priest ventured inside that awful veil (Lev. 16:1, 2; Num. 15, 16). But no sooner was the sacrifice of Christ consummated than the veil was rent from top to bottom (Matt. 27: 51) ; for by His death He glorified God in every attribute of His character concerning the question of sin, and by that one offering perfected for ever them that are sanctified, and the veil was therefore rent to signify that the way was now made open into the holiest of all. "For that which rent the veil in order to admit us has likewise put away the sin which shut us out." It is thus now the privilege of every believer, on the ground of the efficacy of the sacrifice of Christ, to enter at all times into the holiest of all—he has boldness to do so by the blood of Jesus.

But there is a third thing indicated, which may be briefly noticed before calling your attention to the full consequence of these blessed truths; viz., "an high priest over the house of God." And where is our high priest? "Every priest standeth daily ministering and offering oftentimes the same sacrifices, which can never take away sins: but this Man, after He had offered one sacrifice for sins, *for ever sat down on the right hand of God;* from henceforth expecting till His enemies be made His footstool. For by one offering He hath perfected for ever them that are sanctified" (vv. 11-14). We thus learn that our High Priest is seated at the right hand of God, and that this attitude is owing to the fact that His sacrificial work has been accomplished; and hence His presence in heaven is a witness and a proof of the abiding efficacy of His work, and consequently a perpetual encouragement to His people to enter boldly into the holiest of all—inside the rent veil.

Such are the three immense facts—the blood of Jesus, the rent veil, and the high priest over the house of God, to which the Holy Spirit directs our attention before exhorting us to draw near (v. 22). And the place to which we are invited to approach, or into which we are urged to enter, is the holiest— the holy of holies. That is the place which was typified by the holy of holies in the tabernacle in the wilderness, the place into which Christ, as our Representative and Forerunner, has already entered

(Heb. 4: 14; 6: 19,20). *Our place of worship therefore is in the immediate presence of God,* the scene of the ministry on our behalf of Christ, as the High Priest. True that we are down here on the earth as strangers and pilgrims when we think of priesthood. But this earth can never be the scene of our worship; for we have "boldness to enter into the holiest by the blood of Jesus," and there alone can worship be rendered or accepted. Nay; if I would do homage even to the King, I must go to the place where he sits in state to receive it. Much more, if I would worship God I must do so in the place where He sits on His throne, and into which, for this very purpose, He has, in His ineffable grace, given me a title to enter at all times through the precious blood of Christ. There above, therefore, inside the rent veil, in His own immediate presence, and in no other place, must His people worship. And what a marvellous privilege it is, what inexpressible grace, which He has bestowed upon us, that we should enjoy constant liberty of access before Him to bow there in adoration and praise!

> *"Within the holiest of all,*
> *Cleansed by His precious blood,*
> *Before the throne we prostrate fall,*
> *And worship Thee, O God!"*

Having this truth clearly before us, you will see, I am sure, that to speak of a place of worship on earth would tend to obscure the teaching of Scripture and to undermine our privileges. I do not forget that in many cases, as I have said, very little is meant by the phrase; but, on the other hand, in many others it means a great deal, and begets the idea of sacred and consecrated buildings. The Jews had a "worldly sanctuary" (Heb. 9: 1), one that was erected by divine direction, and according to a divine commandment. But to erect a "sanctuary," or a "holy" building, now, is to take Jewish ground, and to ignore the fact that "we have such an High Priest, who is set on the right hand of the throne of the Majesty in the heavens; a minister of the sanctuary, *and of the true tabernacle which the Lord pitched and not man.*" There cannot therefore be a place of worship on earth; and to call a building by such a name is, unconsciously as it may be done, to overlook, to use no stronger word, the believer's place and privilege, and to misrepresent the truth of Christianity.

It may be necessary to allude to one more point; viz., that all believers alike have the same privilege of access into the holiest. The Scriptures, or rather the Scriptures that deal with church truth, know nothing of a sacred order of men, as distinct from their fellow-believers, who enjoy special privileges, with a title to approach God on behalf of others. All believers are alike priests, and all therefore have the same qualification for access to God as worshippers. The passage we have alluded to in the Hebrews (10: 19-22) is decisive upon this question. Mark its terms: "Having therefore, brethren." All alike are addressed, and all are reminded that they have boldness to enter into the holiest by the blood of Jesus. Again the apostle says: "Let *us* draw near"—associating himself with all whom he addresses; because, in truth, he and they alike were on the same footing before God as to worship. It is especially necessary to hold fast this truth in this day of revival of sacerdotalism and its superstitious claims. The two things are connected. If you have an earthly place of worship, you must also have an order of priests; and these two things combined constitute a denial of Christianity. Hence it is incumbent upon us to contend earnestly for the truth once delivered to the saints.

But we must not be content with the doctrine on the subject. The question for our souls is, Do we know what it is to draw near, to worship in, the holiest? I would press this point very solemnly; for nothing short of this will satisfy the heart of Him by whose precious blood it is we have received such an unspeakable privilege. Let us then be satisfied with nothing less than the enjoyment of it. If we had seen Aaron, on the day of atonement, lifting the sacred veil to enter into the awful presence of a holy God, we should have been impressed not only with the solemnity of the act, but also with the wonderful position of favor and nearness to God which he occupied by virtue of his priesthood. All believers now are in that position. May we then know increasingly what it is to be found inside the rent veil, that we may apprehend more fully the efficacy of that one offering which has brought us into God's presence without a spot upon us, and without a veil between.

Believe me, dear ——,

Yours affectionately in Christ,

E. D.

IX.

WORSHIP

My Dear ——:

Having considered the question, Where is our place of worship? we may now proceed to that of worship itself. The Scriptures are very full of instruction upon this subject; and yet, I venture to say, there is scarcely one concerning which there is so much indifference, and even ignorance, amongst professing Christians. I might even go further, and affirm, that its real character is scarcely understood by believers outside of those who are gathered out to the name of Christ. I do not mean, of course, that there are not individuals in all denominations whose joy it is to be found in adoration before God; such have ever existed throughout the history of the Church. But what I contend is, that the collective worship of the saints—or what it is to worship in the assembly—is almost utterly unknown in any of the many denominations of Christendom. For example, in a book, which has obtained a very wide circulation, written by one of the most popular preachers of the day, it is said, in the discussion of this very subject, that listening to sermons is one of the highest forms of worship. The writer supports this extraordinary statement by the allegation that preaching tends to beget the exercise of the holiest desires and aspirations of the soul. That the presentation of truth may lead to worship no one could deny; but a child would easily perceive the difference between the act of worship and listening to the truth. In preaching—if indeed it be God's truth that is being delivered—the servant comes with a message from God to those who listen; in worship, saints are led into the presence of God to present their adoration and praise. The two things are therefore of an entirely and essentially different character.

Nor is prayer worship. This will at once be seen if I say that a suppliant is not a worshipper. Thus if I go to the King with a petition, I am presented before him in that character; but if I am admitted into his presence to render homage, I am no longer a petitioner. So when I unite with other believers in prayer and intercession, we are before God as those who are seeking special blessings; but when we bow before Him in worship, we give rather than receive; we are before Him wanting nothing, but with full hearts overflowing in adoration at His feet.

Thanksgiving is very intimately connected with, if not of the essence of, worship. For thanksgiving is the consequence of blessings received, whether in providence or in redemption. The sense of God's goodness and grace in thus ministering to us, in blessing us with all spiritual blessings in heavenly places in Christ, constrains us to pour out our thanksgivings in His presence; and then, necessarily, we are led to reflect upon the character and attributes of the God who thus delights to surround us with the tokens of His love and care; and consequently thanksgiving passes over into worship.

But in worship—considered in and by itself, in the proper significance of the act—we lose sight of ourselves and our blessings, and are occupied with what God is in Himself, and what He is for us as revealed in Christ. Led by the Holy Spirit, we rise above ourselves, and contemplate God in all His varied attributes and glories (for while "no man hath seen God at any time, the only-begotten Son, who is in the bosom of the Father, He hath declared Him"—John 1: 18) ; and, overwhelmed by the display of His holiness, majesty, love, mercy, and grace, we cannot but bow at His feet, as we render, in and through our Lord Jesus Christ, the homage of our hearts.

This will be seen more clearly if we turn to the teaching of the Scriptures. The woman of Samaria questioned our Lord concerning this subject, or rather as to the place of worship; and in His reply, He vouchsafed to go far beyond the limits of her question. "Jesus saith unto her, Woman, believe me, the hour cometh when ye shall neither in this mountain, nor yet at Jerusalem, worship the Father. Ye worship ye know not what: we know what we worship: for salvation is of the Jews. But the hour cometh, and now is, when the true worshippers shall worship the Father in spirit and in truth: for the Father seeketh such to worship Him. God is a Spirit: and they that worship Him must worship Him in spirit and in truth" (John 4: 21-24). In the first place, our Lord here plainly teaches that there would be henceforward no special place of worship on earth. Jerusalem had been the sacred place where the temple of God had stood—the place to which His people wended year by year from all parts of the land. (See Psalm 122.) But together with the rejection of Christ, their house, hitherto the house of God, was left unto them desolate (Matt. 23: 37-39) ; and never since that time has there been a material house of God upon earth. The Church is now the habitation of God through the Spirit (Eph. 2: 22) ; and our place of worship (as seen in the last letter) is now inside the rent veil, in the immediate presence of God.

Secondly, He tells us who can be worshippers—those who shall worship the Father in spirit and in truth; and such the Father was seeking. That is, only believers, only those whom God in His grace was seeking, such as this woman of Samaria, whom He sought and found in the Person of the Son, and whom He would bring into relationship with Himself as His children; such, and such alone, could worship the Father in spirit and in truth. The apostle affirms the same thing when he says, "We are the circumcision, who worship God in the spirit" (or, as many read, who worship by the Spirit of God), "and rejoice in Christ Jesus, and have no confidence in the flesh," all evident characteristics of believers. Indeed, as the epistle to the Hebrews teaches (see chap. 10), it is impossible for any to approach God until their sins are gone from His sight; and again, without faith (chap. 11: 6); and once more, inasmuch as none but believers have the Spirit of God (see Romans 8: 14-16; Gal. 4: 6), none other can worship in spirit, or by the Spirit of God.

But evident as is this truth, and accepted widely as it is in theory, it needs to be enforced again and again; for, as a matter of fact, in the current "public worship" which obtains on every side, all distinction between believers and unbelievers is either ignored or obliterated. All alike, whether saved or unsaved, are invited to unite in the same prayers, and in the same songs of praise, in utter forgetfulness of these plain words, that it is only the "true worshippers" who can worship the Father in spirit and in truth.

Thirdly, the Lord defines the character of worship. It must be "in spirit and in truth." "Now to worship 'in spirit' is to worship according to the true nature of God, and in the power of that communion which the Spirit of God gives. Spiritual worship is thus in contrast with the forms and ceremonies, and all the religiousness of which the flesh is capable. To worship God 'in truth' is to worship Him according to the revelation which He has given of Himself. The Samaritans worshipped God neither in spirit nor in truth. The Jews worshipped God in truth, so far as this can be said, of a revelation which was imperfect; but they worshipped Him in no respect *in spirit*. Now to worship God, both are needful. He is to be worshipped according to the true revelation of Himself (that is, 'in truth'), and according to His nature (that is, 'in spirit')."

But the revelation of God to us is in the Person, and connected with the work of Christ; for all that God is has been manifested in and through the cross. The death of Christ is therefore the foundation of all Christian worship; for it is by the efficacy of His precious blood that we are qualified to enter into the presence of God, and inasmuch as that death is the revelation to us of all that God is, of His majesty, His holiness, His truth, His grace, and His love, it is through the contemplation of that wondrous sacrifice that our hearts, wrought upon by the Spirit of God, are led out in adoration and praise. Thus worship is connected in a very special way with the Lord's table, because it is when we are gathered around it, as members of the body of Christ, that we show forth His death. To quote once more the words of another, "It is impossible to separate true spiritual worship and communion from the perfect offering of Christ to God. The moment our worship separates itself from its efficacy, and the consciousness of that infinite acceptance of Jesus before the Father, it becomes carnal, and either a form or delight of the flesh."

This is the secret of the degeneration of worship in Christendom; for wherever the Lord's Table has lost its true character or place, the spring and motive of worship are obscured. For what are we specially reminded of at the table of the Lord? It is His death; and it is in that death we are enabled to see what God is for us, and what Christ is to God, as well as the infinite efficacy of His sacrifice in bringing us without a spot into God's immediate presence —in the light as He is in the light. The grace, the eternal love of God, and the grace and the unquenchable love of Christ, are alike displayed to our souls, as we remember the One who glorified God in His death on the cross, where He bore our sins; and having boldness to enter the holiest by the blood of Jesus, we bow and worship before God, as we sing—

> "O God! Thou now hast glorified
>   Thy holy, blest, eternal Son;
> The Nazarene, the Crucified,
>   Now sits exalted on Thy throne!
> To Him in faith we cry aloud,
>   Worthy art Thou, O Lamb of God."

Leaving you to trace out the subject from the hints we have given,

Believe me, dear ——,

Yours affectionately in Christ,

E. D.

X.

MINISTRY

My Dear ——:

It is a most remarkable fact, that the ministry which obtains among the "churches" of Christendom has not even a show of justification from the word of God. Search as closely as you may, from the time of the Church of God was constituted until the close of the inspired record, you will not find a trace of the "one-man" ministry. Apostles, elders or bishops, deacons, pastors and teachers, and evangelists are mentioned; but there is no indication of anything to correspond with the ministers and preachers of the present day. For all the denominations of Christendom—with one or two unimportant exceptions—agree in their theory of the ministry. One man is, as a rule, appointed to take the charge or oversight of a "church" and congregation; and he is expected to teach, to preach the gospel, and to be a pastor. In short, he is expected to unite in himself the office of an elder, and the gifts of a pastor and teacher, and of an evangelist. It will thus often happen that one man will have the sole and continued charge of the same congregation for twenty, thirty, or forty years; and it cannot be denied that professing Christians love to have it so.

But the question is, Is this practice scriptural? Bear with me a little, while I seek to answer this question from the word of God. I need scarcely remind you that our blessed Lord appointed apostles during His earthly sojourn; and that, after His resurrection and ascension, He appeared to Saul, and also chose and made him in an especial way the apostle of the Gentiles. (See Acts 9, 22, 26; 1 Cor. 15.)

Now the apostles, as all confess, had a peculiar and an unique place—having been endowed with extraordinary gifts and authority—*and they never had successors*. I shall not detain you long upon this point, as apart from the Romish and Anglican Churches* (at least in the West) this statement would be generally accepted. Two Scriptures will therefore suffice. Peter, writing to the believers of his own nation—"the strangers scattered throughout Pontus" etc.—says, "I will endeavor" (*i.e.*, by writing the epistle) "that ye may be able *after my decease* to have these things always in remembrance" (2 Peter 1: 15). He thus commits them in the future to the guidance (not of apostolic successors, but) of the written word. Paul, in like manner, addressing the elders of the Church in Ephesus, and warning them of their coming difficulties and dangers, says, "And now, brethren, I commend you to God, and to the word of His grace" (Acts 20: 32). The two great apostles therefore—one of the circumcision, and the other of the uncircumcision, agree in this—that they alike declare that the resource of the Church, after they should have passed away, would be in the word of God. It is thus clear that they could not have contemplated successors to their office.

The next office in order will be that of bishops or elders. I say bishops or elders, because in fact they

* See foot note on Page 30.

are but two names for the same office. This is
proved beyond dispute from Acts 20. We there read
that Paul sent for "the elders of the church" (v. 17).
In speaking to them, he terms them "overseers" (v.
28)—*i.e.*, bishops (ἐπισκόπους). Well, these are
never found alone. The Church at Ephesus, in the
passage before us, had more than one. Paul called
the "elders" of the Church. So too in Acts 14: 23,
Paul and Barnabas "ordained them elders in every
city." In the epistle to the Philippians also we
read of "the bishops and deacons" (1: 1; see also
Acts 15: 23; Titus 1: 5).

Passing now to the gifts, as distinguished from
office, we come to "pastors and teachers" (Eph. 4:
11). I have put the two together because, in fact,
they are so linked in the Scriptures, and linked in
so close a way in the passage just cited, as to indicate that they may be united in the same person.
Are these, then, ever found alone, having the charge
of a congregation? So far from this being the case,
we are told that "there were in the Church that was
at Antioch certain prophets and teachers," and the
names of no less than five are given (Acts 13: 1).

Should it, however, be thought that the cases of
Timothy and Titus are evidence on the other side, a
moment's consideration will dispel the illusion. Titus
is told plainly that he was left in Crete to "set in
order the things that were wanting, and to ordain
elders in every city" (Titus 1: 5); and Timothy is
directed as to the qualifications of such (1 Tim. 3),
and expressly told "to lay hands suddenly on no
man" (v. 22); *i.e.*, to appoint them to office. Nothing therefore can be plainer than that these two,
Timothy and Titus, were acting as delegates of the
apostle, and as such exercised a general supervision,

and had authority to appoint suited men to the office of bishops and deacons; an authority employed, be it remarked, by individuals, not by churches, and which was never exercised but by the apostles, or, as in the case before us, by their delegates, and which was never transmitted to any successors, and consequently lapsed with the death of the apostles.

One other gift remains to be noticed—that of the evangelist (Eph. 4: 11). It comes after "prophets," but we have reserved it because of its character. As the name imports, the work of an evangelist is to preach the gospel; and hence the object of his ministry is not the Church, but the world. Our Lord Himself describes the responsibility of the evangelist when He commands His apostles, "Go ye into all the world, and preach the gospel to every creature" (Mark 16: 15). To confine him therefore in his service to a single congregation, or even a single town or city, would be to ignore the object of the gift. Hence St. Paul, speaking of himself in this character, says, "I am debtor both to the Greeks, and to the barbarians; both to the wise, and to the unwise. So, as much as in me is, I am ready to preach the gospel to you that are at Rome also" (Rom. 1: 14, 15).

The question then recurs, What is the true character of ministry according to the word of God? In the first place, it flows from Christ at the right hand of God, as the Head of the Church. He is its source. "But unto every one of us is given grace according to the measure of the gift of Christ. Wherefore He saith, When He ascended up on high, He led captivity captive, and gave gifts unto men. . . . And He gave some, apostles; and some, prophets;

and some, evangelists; and 'some, pastors and teachers; for the perfecting of the saints, for the work of the ministry, for the edifying of the body of Christ: till we all come in the unity of the faith and of the knowledge of the Son of God, unto a perfect man, unto the measure of the stature of the fulness of Christ," etc. (Eph. 4: 7-13). This affords us a most important principle. The gifts were not bestowed upon the Church, but upon men for the benefit of the Church. Hence those who have received them are responsible for their exercise, not to the Church, but to the Lord. It is impossible therefore for the Church to appoint pastors and teachers, or any of the gifts named, seeing indeed that the responsibility of the Church is to receive the ministry of every one who has been qualified by the Lord for its edification. Even as the apostolic office of St. Paul, so a gift is "not of men, neither by man" (Gal. 1: 1), but it is from the risen Christ.

There is another truth of equal moment; viz., that the gifts can only be properly exercised in the power of the Holy Spirit. The presence of the Holy Ghost is the distinctive characteristic of this dispensation. He dwells in the house of God—the Church, and He dwells in believers (John 7: 39; 14: 16, 17; Acts 2; Rom. 8: 15, 16; 1 Cor. 6: 19; 2 Cor. 6: 16; Eph. 1: 13; 2: 22; etc.). Hence when believers are gathered together, as 1 Cor. 12 to 14 teaches, He acts sovereignly in and through the members of the body of Christ according to their gift: "For to one is given by the Spirit the word of wisdom; to another the word of knowledge by the same Spirit. . . . But all these worketh that one and the selfsame Spirit, dividing to every man severally as He will" (1 Cor.

12: 8-11). Any human arrangement for ministry therefore in the assembly is not only inconsistent with this truth, but it utterly ignores the prerogative of the Spirit of God to minister by whom He will. Surely a most solemn thing, and not to be lightly thought of; and yet, alas, how common! Nay more, so entirely is the presence of the Holy Ghost forgotten, that man's authority, and man's claims, are substituted, justified, and accepted by the mass of professing Christians.

You will be careful to observe that what the Scripture teaches is not that all have liberty to minister, but that there should be liberty to the Holy Ghost to minister by whom He may please. There is a wide difference between the two things. The first would be democracy, than which there is nothing more alien from the mind of God; the second involves the maintenance of the Lordship of Christ in the power of the Spirit, the subjection of all the members of the body to the Head, and complete dependence upon the guidance and wisdom of the Spirit of God. In the first, man is prominent; in the second, Christ is owned as supreme.

While asserting these cardinal principles of ministry, we must be careful to recollect that all true ministry must be in subjection to, and in accordance with, the word of God. This clearly follows from the instructions in 1 Cor 14. The apostle indeed gives directions concerning the exercise of the gifts, and afterwards says, "If any man think himself to be a prophet, or spiritual, let him acknowledge that the things that I write unto you are the commandments of the Lord" (v. 37). The assembly is thus entitled, nay, responsible, to judge whether the thing ministered is according to truth

(1 Cor. 14:29), and to reject everything that does not answer to the test. It is not left therefore at the mercy of wilful men, but is furnished with a safeguard sufficient to hold in check and to rebuke all that savors of the flesh, and not of the Spirit.

Another thing may be added. After dealing with the question of gifts, and pointing out that even their exercise are utterly valueless without charity (love) (1 Cor. 12, 13), the apostle teaches that the object of their exercise is the edification of the assembly (14:3-5). How beautiful are the ways of God! Gathered by the Spirit around the person of our Lord at His table, to show forth His death, He leads our hearts out in adoration and praise, and then He ministers to us from God through various members of the body of Christ. There is thus a double action of the Spirit. He enables us to offer the sacrifices of praise to God; and mindful of our need, He gives the word of wisdom, or knowledge, or exhortation, as our state may require.

But I have reached the limits of my letter. You will, however, be able to trace out the subject for yourself, and thus discover whether what has been advanced is according to the word of God. "Prove all things; hold fast that which is good" (1 Thess. 5:21).

Believe me, dear ——,

Yours affectionately in Christ,

E. D.

P.S.—In addition to the scriptures cited, read Romans 12:4-8; 1 Peter 4:10, 11, etc.

XI

THE WORD OF GOD

My Dear —:

It is impossible to lay too much stress upon the importance and value of the Word of God. Love for it, indeed, should be a characteristic of every believer; and it were not too much to say that our growth in grace, and in the knowledge of our Lord and Saviour Jesus Christ, is largely connected with it. Take for example Psalm 119, and you will see how it is bound up with every phase of the spiritual life of the psalmist. Some of his expressions might well humble us, as they reveal to us the place the Word occupied in his affections. He says, "I will delight myself in Thy statutes: I will not forget Thy Word"; again, "Thy testimonies also are my delight and my counsellors"; and again, "I will delight myself in Thy commandments, which I have loved" (vv. 16, 24, 47). In still stronger language he exclaims, "O how love I Thy law! it is my meditation all the day"; and once more, "I love Thy commandments above gold; yea, above fine gold" (vv. 97, 127). Job, in like manner says, "I have esteemed the words of His mouth more than my necessary food" (23: 12). And from that time to this the same characteristic has ever been found in all earnest, devout, and spiritual minds. I propose then to bring before you in this letter some of the many aspects in which the Word of God is presented, in relation to the believer.

1. It is the instrumentality of the new birth. "Of His own will begat He us with the Word of truth." (Jas. 1: 18). "Being born again, not of corruptible

seed, but of incorruptible, by the Word of God, which liveth and abideth for ever" (1 Peter 1: 23). Our Lord teaches the same truth when He says that "a man must be born of water and the Spirit" (John 3); for water is a well-known symbol of the Word.

2. As it is the instrumentality of the new birth, so is it also the proper aliment for the new nature. St. Peter thus says: "As newborn babes, desire the sincere milk of the Word, that ye may grow thereby," (many copies add, "up to salvation"); "if so be ye have tasted that the Lord is gracious" (1 Peter 2: 2, 3). Again we are told that "man doth not live by bread only, but by every word which proceedeth out of the mouth of the Lord doth man live" (Deut. 8: 3; Matt. 4: 4). The Word therefore is the suited food and sustenance for the spiritual life, the means of our nourishment and strength in Christ, as we journey on through the wilderness, waiting for the Lord's return, or to depart and be with Himself, which is far better. I say in Christ, because, as you know, Christ Himself is our food, both as the manna and the old corn of the land, and indeed, to go further back, as the lamb roast with fire (Exodus 12); but then it is only in the word of God that He is unfolded to us thus in these several characters. If we would collect the manna for our daily use, we have to roam through the gospels and epistles, where we find Him especially presented to us in this aspect—as a humbled Christ in incarnation; and then, if I would feed upon Him as the old corn of the land, upon a glorified Christ, I am led to the epistles (e.g., Col. 3; Phil. 3, etc.) which present Him as such to our souls. The Scriptures therefore are the green pastures into which the Good Shepherd would lead His flock.

3. It is our only guide. "Thy Word is a lamp unto my feet, and a light unto my path" (Psalm 119: 105). So, when Joshua was about to lead Israel into Canaan, the Lord said unto him, "Only be thou strong and very courageous that thou mayest observe to do according to all the law, which Moses My servant commanded thee: turn not from it to the right hand or to the left, that thou mayest prosper whithersoever thou goest. This book of the law shall not depart out of thy mouth; but thou shalt meditate therein day and night, that thou mayest observe to do according to all that is written therein: for then thou shalt make thy way prosperous, and then thou shalt have good success" (Joshua 1: 7, 8). So in the New Testament, as well as in the Old, the Word of God is everywhere indicated as our only guide as we pass through this tangled scene.

"Pillar of fire, through watches dark,
    And radiant cloud by day;
When waves would whelm our tossing bark,
    Our anchor and our stay."

(See Acts 20: 32; 2 Thess. 3: 14; 2 Tim. 3: 15-17; 2 Peter 1: 15; 1 John 2: 27; Jude 3, etc.)

4. It is our means of defence against the temptations and wiles of Satan; hence it is called the sword of the Spirit (Ephes. 6: 17). We thus see in the temptation of our blessed Lord that it was His only weapon. To all the allurements which Satan presented to His soul—and he assailed Him through every avenue of approach, and in every character— He replied, "It is written." From first to last, He never expressed a thought of His own, but rested for His defence entirely and alone upon the Word

of God. Satan consequently was utterly powerless; he could not advance a single step; but, defeated at every point, he had to retire baffled and overcome. And he is as powerless today as then, when encountered in the same way. He cannot touch an obedient, dependent man. Would that every young believer, indeed all, whether young or old, might always bear it in mind!

5. It is the only standard of doctrine or practice. We have therefore to test everything presented to us by the Word. Thus in the letters to the seven churches we find in every case, "He that hath an ear, let him hear what the Spirit saith to the churches." They and their practices were alike to be measured by this infallible standard. In like manner, the apostle Paul continually reminds those to whom he writes of their responsibility of gauging everything by what he had taught. (See, for example, Galatians 1: 8, 9; 1 Cor. 15:1-11; 2 Thess. 2: 15; 3: 14.)

6. It is the means of our practical holiness. Our Lord thus prays, when He presented His own before the Father: "Sanctify them through Thy truth: Thy Word is truth" (John 17: 17). It is only indeed by constant application of the Word to ourselves, our walk, and our ways, that we are increasingly separated from evil; just as it is by the application of the Word through the Spirit that the Lord, as our Advocate with the Father, washes the feet of His own. This is the work which He in His grace has undertaken for us; but we must never forget the responsibility on our side of continually judging ourselves by the Word in the presence of God. How many a trial and chastening would be spared us if we were more faithful in this particular!

"For if we would judge ourselves, we should not be judged" (1 Cor. 11: 31). Thus the psalmist asks, "Wherewithal shall a young man cleanse his way?" And the answer is, "By taking heed thereto according to Thy Word" (Ps. 119: 9). Again he says, "By the word of Thy lips I have kept me from the paths of the destroyer" (Ps. 17: 4). For it is only from the Scripture that we learn the will of God; and by the application of the Word in the power of the Spirit we are separated, on the one side, from that which is contrary to His mind, and we are brought, on the other, into conformity with it; and this being a constant process, we are ever attaining increasing holiness, the perfection of which is only found in the glorified Christ at God's right hand.

7. Last of all, I would remind you of the value which the Lord sets upon obedience to the Word. Take, for instance, the familiar scripture, "If any man love Me, he will keep My Word: and My Father will love him, and We will come unto him, and make our abode with him" (John 14: 23). See how large a blessing is made dependent upon our keeping His Word; for it should never be overlooked that the love of the Father in this passage, and the Father and the Son coming to make their abode with us, are entirely conditional. Again, in the next chapter, He says, "If ye keep My commandments, ye shall abide in My love; even as I have kept My Father's commandments, and abide in His love" 15: 10). Once more, not to multiply citations, at the very close of the inspired record He says, "Behold, I come quickly: blessed is he that keepeth the sayings of the prophecy of this book" (Rev. 22: 7). Thus He not only expects us to prize and treasure up the communications which He has deigned to

make to us; but He also counts upon our hearts to delight in obedience to every Word that has proceeded out of His mouth; yea, He has made obedience to be the highest expression of our love. "If ye love Me, keep My commandments" (John 14: 15).

From this rapid outline of some of the uses, and some of our responsibilities in respect of the Word of God, you will at least recognize its supreme importance to the believer. Allow me, then, to make one or two practical observations which may be helpful to you and other young Christians. First of all, you will see the necessity of being familiar with the Scriptures. For instance, I could not repel a temptation, as the Saviour did, unless I were acquainted with the scripture wherewith to meet it. In like manner, there might be many cases in which I should be led astray simply from not knowing that the Lord had revealed His mind in His Word. One of the first obligations, therefore, of the believer is to study the Word of God. "My son, if thou wilt receive my words, and hide my commandments with thee; so that thou incline thine ear unto wisdom, and apply thine heart to understanding; yea, if thou criest after knowledge, and liftest up thy voice for understanding; if thou seekest her as silver, and searchest for her as for hid treasures; then shalt thou understand the fear of the Lord, and find the knowledge of God. For the Lord giveth wisdom: out of His mouth cometh knowledge and understanding" (Prov. 2: 1-6). In this spirit you must search and systematically study the Scriptures, if you would be "throughly furnished unto all good works" (2 Tim. 3: 17). I do not say, Read no other book; but I do say, Make the Bible your chief companion, and confine yourself as much as possible to those books which help you to understand it; for it should be the chief aim of every believer to be thoroughly conversant with the mind and will of God. Secondly, let me counsel you, if you read much, to meditate more. "The slothful man roasteth not that which he took in hunting" (Prov. 12: 27). He finds his pleasure in the chase, and once finding, obtaining, he is satisfied. It is thus with many in reading the Word. Their delight is in the acquisition of truth; and in this they rest, and thereby lose the blessing. In the scripture already cited, the Lord said to Joshua, "This book of the law shall not depart out of thy mouth; but thou shalt meditate therein day and night" (See also Ps. 1: 2; 119: 97; Prov: 22:17, 18; 1 Tim. 4: 15, etc). For it is in meditation in the presence of the Lord that the sweetness, beauty, and power of the Word are unfolded to us. Never, therefore, lose an opportunity for meditation on the scripture you may read. And, lastly, always remember your entire dependence upon the Spirit of God for the understanding of the Word. "For what man knoweth the things of a man, save the spirit of man which is in him? even so the things of God knoweth no man, but the Spirit of God. Now we have received, not the spirit of the world, but the Spirit which is of God; that we might know the things that are freely given to us of God" (1 Cor. 2: 11, 12).

If you thus read the Scriptures, you will be led daily into increasing acquaintance with the truth, and thereby be drawn into closer fellowship with the Father and His Son Jesus Christ.

Believe me, dear ——,

Yours affectionately in Christ, E. D.

XII.

PRAYER

My Dear ——:

There remains only one other subject to bring before you in this present series of letters. In the last I directed you to the importance of the Word of God, and now I desire to speak of prayer and its connection with the spiritual life. These two—the Word of God and prayer—are ever conjoined. It was so in the blessed activities of the life of our Lord. After a long day of ministry we find such a record as this, "And He withdrew Himself into the wilderness, and prayed"; and again, "It came to pass in those days, that He went out into a mountain to pray, and continued all night in prayer to God" (Luke 5:16; 6:12). So, too, when the difficulty arose in the Pentecostal church concerning the distribution of the offerings of the saints, the apostle said, "It is not reason that we should leave the Word of God, and serve tables. . . . We will give ourselves continually to prayer, and to the ministry of the Word" (Acts 6:2-4). St. Paul likewise unites the two things in his description of the whole armour of God; for no sooner has he said, "And take the helmet of salvation, and the sword of the Spirit, which is the Word of God," than he adds, "Praying always with all prayer and supplication in the Spirit" (Eph. 6:17, 18).

We have, moreover, direct exhortations to prayer; as for example, "Continuing instant in prayer";

"Pray without ceasing" (Rom. 12:12; 1 Thess. 5:17. See also Luke 18, etc.). And if you read the introductory parts of St. Paul's epistles you will see how he embodied his own exhortations. As you trace his path, as recorded for us in the Acts, you would think that he never did anything else than preach; but if you read these parts of the epistles you would almost think that he never did anything else than pray. Approximating to the example of our blessed Lord in his unwearied labours, he found, yea, he *learnt*, the need of constant waiting upon God. In like manner, prayer is a necessity for every child of God. For we are in ourselves weak and helpless, entirely dependent; and prayer is but the expression of our dependence on Him to whom we pray. Dependent upon God for everything, our very needs urge us into His presence; and having liberty of access through Christ, because of the place we occupy, and because of the relationship we enjoy, we "come boldly unto the throne of grace, that we may obtain mercy, and find grace to help in time of need" (Heb. 4: 16).

1. Our Lord teaches what should be, so to speak, the manner of our prayers. Speaking to His disciples of the time when He should be absent from them, He says, "Whatsoever ye shall ask *in My name*, that will I do," etc.; and again, "If ye shall ask any thing *in My name*, I will do it" (John 14: 13, 14). Two things are here involved. The name of Christ is our warrant to come before God, before the Father, reminding us that our title of approach is in Christ alone. And surely this gives us confidence. If we were to think only of ourselves, our failures and unworthiness, we should never venture into God's presence; but when our

eyes are directed to Christ, what He is in Himself, what He is to God, and what He is to us,· and remembering that we appear before God in all His infinite acceptability, we are made to understand that God delights in us—in our approach, in our cries and prayers. We thus are encouraged to draw near to God, and to pour out our hearts before Him in every time of trial or need.

But asking in the name of Christ is more than having a title through His name; it is, indeed, to appear before God with all the value and authority of that name. If, for example, I go to a bank and present a check, I ask for the value of the check in the name of him by whom it is drawn. So when I appear before God in the name of Christ, I present my supplications in all the value of that name to God. Hence it is that our Lord says, "If ye shall ask any thing in My name, I will do it," because, indeed, it is the joy of the heart of God to grant every request that is so preferred. The promise is absolute, without any limitation; for the simple reason that nothing could be asked in the name of Christ which was not in accordance with the will of God. For we could not use His name for any request which was not begotten in our hearts by His own Spirit.

2. In the next chapter our Lord gives us further teaching on the same subject. "If ye abide in Me, and My words abide in you, ye shall ask what ye will, and it shall be done unto you" (John 15: 7). We may connect with this another scripture: "And this is the confidence that we have in Him, that, if we ask anything according to His will, He heareth us" (1 John 5: 14). Here it is according to the will of God, thereby excluding everything which is

not of this character. But our Lord says, "What ye will"; and this brings before us a very important aspect of prayer. In this case it is conditional: "If ye abide in Me, and My words abide in you"; that is, abiding in Christ, ever remembering our dependence upon Him for everything, that without Him we can do nothing; and His words abiding in us, moulding us after His own mind, forming Himself in us, we of necessity express His own thoughts and His own desires, and consequently "what we will" must, in such a case, be "according to *His* will." It will be seen, at the same time, that the power of our prayers depends upon our spiritual condition. This is an unfailing principle. It is stated by St. John: "If our heart condemn us not, [then] have we confidence toward God. And whatsoever we ask, we receive of Him, because we keep His commandments, and do those things that are pleasing in His sight" (1 John 3: 21, 22). St. James also tells us, "The effectual fervent prayer of a righteous man availeth much" (James 5: 16). This is of all importance; for neglecting our spiritual state, and thereby losing present communion with God, our prayers become cold and lifeless, degenerate into a repetition of known truths or old phrases, and thus, losing all significance, pass over into dead forms. The words are uttered to satisfy conscience; but expressing no heart-felt needs, and no outgoings of soul after God, they find no response, and bring down no blessing. Beware of such a state, which is often the commencement of the backslider's path, and which, unless checked by the grace of God, will land the soul in open shame and dishonor to the name of Christ.

3. The uses of prayer are manifold. In the first place, the Lord has associated us with Himself in all

His own desires. Yea, our fellowship is with the Father, and with His Son Jesus Christ (1 John 1:3). God therefore counts upon our love to have fellowship with all that is dear to His own heart. He has made His interests ours; and consequently He would have us enter into and make these the object of our prayers. What a privilege! To be permitted to range through all His purposes as revealed to us in the Word; to watch with delight their unfoldings; to behold them all centering in, and radiating from, the person of His Christ, as well as bringing back a revenue of glory to His name! Truly if we are enabled to enter at all into this wondrous position, by the power of the Spirit, we shall lack neither subject for, nor motive to, prayer.

Then, too, we may express in prayer all the manifold needs of our own souls. "Be careful for nothing; but in every thing by prayer and supplication with thanksgiving let your requests be made known unto God. And the peace of God, which passeth all understanding, shall keep your hearts and minds through Christ Jesus" (Phil. 4: 6, 7). This word is the more remarkable from the fact that it is found in the very chapter in which the apostle assures us, "My God shall supply all your need according to His riches in glory by Christ Jesus" (v. 19). Still, notwithstanding this blessed confidence, God would have us, with all the freedom of children, to make known to Him our requests; and though He does not promise to grant them in every case, He yet assures us that His peace shall guard our hearts. It is in this way, indeed, that confidence is established in our intercourse with God, that the priceless habit is formed of having no reserves with Him, and that intimacy of communion is cultivated. It is in accordance with this that the psalmist cries, "Trust in Him at all times; ye people, *pour out your heart before Him*" (Psalm 62: 8) ; and that St. Peter says, "Casting all your care upon Him; for He careth for you" (1 Peter 5: 7).

4. It should be added that the word of God lays great stress upon the connection of faith with prayer. Our Lord says, "What things soever ye desire, when ye pray, believe that ye receive them, and ye shall have them" (Mark 11: 24). St. James also, after his exhortation to ask wisdom of God, says, "Let him ask in faith, nothing wavering" (1: 6) ; and again, he tells us that "the prayer of *faith* shall save the sick" (5: 15). So too in the Hebrews we read, that "without faith it is impossible to please Him: for he that cometh" (*i.e.*, draws near) "to God must believe that He is, and that He is a rewarder of them that diligently seek Him" (11: 6). This is easy to understand; for surely God has a right to count upon our confidence in His love, our trust in His character, and our belief in His word, since He has so fully revealed Himself to us in the person of His Son. To doubt, therefore, as we approach Him, would be to dishonor His name. And just as He counts upon our confidence and faith, He would have us count upon His faithfulness and love. As our blessed Lord reminds His disciples, "Your Father knoweth what things ye have need of, before ye ask Him" (Matt. 6: 8). And as St. Paul teaches us, "He that spared not His own Son, but delivered Him up for us all, how shall He not with Him also freely give us all things?" (Rom. 8: 32). Thus the gift of His own Son, inasmuch as it was His greatest gift, and the most perfect pledge of His love, is the foundation on which we may rest in the

full assurance that He not only will not withhold any good thing from us, but that He will delight to bless us according to His own heart, and according to His own knowledge of our need.

5. Once more, all true prayer must be in and by the Holy Spirit. ((See Rom. 8: 26, 27; Phil. 3: 3; Jude 20). Indeed, He is the power for prayer, as He is for every activity of the spiritual life. We are thus utterly dependent upon the Lord Jesus for access to God, upon the Holy Spirit for power to pray, and upon God for the blessings we seek. To His name be all the praise!

But .I will not pursue the subject further. You will, however, permit me to urge upon you perseverance in prayer. Rules on such a subject—as to times and frequency—we have no right to make or impose. Still of one thing be very sure—*you cannot be too much in prayer*. And if you dwell in the presence of God, you will find both the heart and occasion for prayer. Our responsibility is to pray without ceasing, always maintaining uninterruptedly the consciousness of dependence, and our need of divine grace. Thus we shall be always cast upon God, always enjoy liberty of heart in His presence, and consequently be always finding, in the constant reception of mercies, grace and blessing, in answer to our cries, new themes for thanksgiving and praise.

Believe me dear ——,

Yours affectionately in Christ,

E. D.